A handbook to keep a Joy Warrior strong
(in case a pandemic erupts)

by jennifer robinson

Warrior Strong:

A Handbook to Keep a Joy Warrior Strong (in case a pandemic erupts)

By Jennifer Robinson

Copyright 2021

ALL RIGHTS RESERVED

No part of this publication may be reproduced, stored in a retrieval system, or transmitted, in any form or by any means—electronic, mechanical, photocopying, recording or otherwise—without prior written permission.

ISBN 978-1-7351760-5-5

Personal Chapters, LLC
Independence, Missouri and Wakarusa, KS
personalchapters@gmail.com

Dedication

I dedicate this book and all my new adventures, to the JOY that continues to live in our beautiful world. There are wonderfully dynamic people around every corner with a story, a song, or a beautiful message of hope…people waiting to share a simple encounter with strangers for no reason at all. To me, this is JOY living out loud!

Many of these people are members of my tribe. They continue to be my "hand-picked" family, from both near and far. Whether we speak each week or just twice a year, every one of you is the part of my heart that keeps me WARRIOR STRONG.

To my "God given" family, your hugs are never ending and your love is everlasting. I am forever blessed to be a member of our huge team. My soul radiates joy because of all you have given to my life!

"I have found the one whom my soul loves" Song of Solomon 3:4.

Thank you, Darryl Edward. I know this quote was written to light up, in bright Las Vegas neon lights, the love we share. Thank you for our countless trips to anywhere and everywhere, for our deep and sometimes "aqua lung" conversations, constant laughter and walks with Leo. We are having a wonderful journey together as life partners, riding our bikes into any sunset we can find!

I am a self-proclaimed Joy Warrior. I am a collector of memories and moments in time in which we can share love and laughter. After walking over 50 years in my size 9 shoes, I have earned a badge of honor. I know I am Warrior Strong! Let's sit together for a while and I can tell you how all of this accidently happened to me….

Prologue

The year 2018 was electric from beginning to end.

If we are lucky, there are moments in our lives we cannot believe we have the good fortune to be a part of. The year 2018 was that year for me. Then, just like a great record playing over and over, the hits kept on coming. Then the year 2019 came in with brilliance and illumination and ended with inspiration for the new decade we were about to enter.

I remember taking many weeks prior to the end of 2019 to pause and contemplate, and to appreciate how quickly time had moved from 2010 to the now impending 2020. An entire decade moved at the speed of light. I recalled many memories and moments that were made and shared. They showered my heart with feelings like the deep blue water from the oceans I connect with so intensely.

Time is a funny treasure. We constantly collect it, just like we collect the oxygen we breathe. We don't notice how we are dependent on it for survival until it stops or is stolen from us. In my daily journeys through life, as time continues moving forward. I find myself collecting stories and conversations. I catalogue these in my mind using an intricate type of Dewey Decimal system to ensure that they are all captured, ready to be pulled and retold. I had no idea that all these occasions of collecting were setting the stage for me to put on my warrior suit and once again step up to the game of life.

I did not know or understand this moment in time would test my fortitude in a way that could not be defined. As a JOY warrior, I am strong and I carry my suit with me at all times. But wait! Did I miss a Zoom meeting? Were there continuing education classes that I did not get invited to? I felt to my core that my journey thus far kept me insulated from the outside world. I even felt that my lifetime expedition had prepared me for any occasion that would or could arrive. But then, like digits on a Casio watch, the numbers 3.13.2020 rolled over and changed everything.

A couple more stories...

2.1
JOY, just open yourself then quickly quarantine. 7

2.2
Can't change your past, change your perspective and then your team will win the Super Bowl! 15

2.3
Let your inside light shine bright; it will glow from your shaved head! 20

2.4
"Separately, United; we are alone together!" We became a country western song! 26

2.5
Plant seeds of hope, ground yourself and then water with gin and tonic... 32

2.6
While going through a spiritual expedition, can you earn mileage? 39

2.7
Giving is not seasonal; neither is toilet paper............................ 44

2.8
How do I listen to the whispers?! Is that stored in my iCloud?..59

2.9
"I am OPEN. I can see farther than my eyes can look!"...........56

2.1

JOY: Just Open Yourself.... Then Quickly Quarantine!

"I had to suit up in 2013. I had to put on my warrior suit and fight many battles to stay alive. Because of this experience I approach every day as if it is a new event. I am here. I have my purpose. I am calm. I listen to the whispers in the universe. I am kind. I am quiet. I am grateful. I am mindful. I am BOLD and I am strong. I am enough.

I do not need to be perfect, because I am whole. I keep the imaginary red balloons around me at all times, keeping out the crazy. Most importantly, my new career in life is to live my truth and my own self-worth. I am a self-proclaimed JOY Warrior."

I wrote a tiny little book in 2018. **JOY Warrior** was created from my journey as a survival guide. It was written as an example of optimal living in joy when you become half of your whole, as I did in battling cancer and chronic Lyme Disease. I shared my stories to ease the pain that we can feel when walking through our own silent wars. I wanted to help complete strangers in any way I could, perhaps allowing someone to simply sleep through the night.

I could not have predicted, not even using the best algorithms or the best bookie in Vegas, that two short years later I would be tested again. In fact, we all would be tested in ways no one could imagine. Once again I had to pull out my warrior suit and fight battles just to stay alive.

But before I tell that story, let's walk back 24 short months. We have so much to catch up on, my friend...

warrior strong

To know me is to know that I love to travel. I simply enjoy the privilege of being able to go somewhere, anywhere, at almost a moment's notice. I love planning where to go and what to do, and love seeking out local vendors for food and fun. I even enjoy the packing and unpacking of specific items for just the holiday or specific trip I'm on. I even love the notion that a hotel becomes a temporary home away from home. In fact, this entire ritual gives me great JOY!

I ran into 2018 quite literally. I began running in August of 2017 and participated in several 5K runs a month, finding excitement in this new normal in my life. I was healthy again and knew I could conquer this challenge. I did not finish any race first, or even 100th in my age group. The goal every time I heard the gun go off was to finish the race, no matter what. I knew there would be a really cool medal at the end that I would wear and share on social media as I marked it off the list as another race done.

The month of January 2019 ended with my birthday. There I was, at 49 years young, running in a race.

Days after beginning my new trip around the sun, I glanced at the calendar in early February and suddenly remembered that my mother had been gone from us for five years. I don't know what upset me more… that mom was not here to celebrate all the special occasions that she loved so much, or the fact that five years had moved like sand through my hands. This moment stopped me in my tracks. I listened to the whispers and paid attention to my breathing, and to how I felt and how sad my heart still was. I miss my mother every day and it is an ache that does not ever heal.

In March of 2018 I had a small stem cell procedure on my knee due to damage from the Lyme disease. It was during my healing time that I wrote *Joy Warrior.* I wrote the book in about a week as a complete download of all I had been through and survived since 2013. It was cathartic, healing, emotional and, most of all, reminded me that my ability to insert proper punctuation was severely lacking. (A HUGE thank you to Anne, my dear editor, for helping me to appear much smarter than I am. I am truly grateful!)

Now that I had not been running for a while, I needed to fill my space with road trips with my tribe; trips full of laughter and JOY.

We went to Virginia to see my best friend Trang. Next it was a girls' trip to Ocean City to my best friend Carla's beach house. We had barely disembarked from the plane when my dad and his wife Linda, my daughter Maddison and I went to New York City for a week. That trip was magic; purely delightful. Then came August and the love of my life, Darryl, turned 50 years young and we were "Rockin 50!" for an entire weekend of parties and festivities with our dearest friends and family. Then we took the band on the road and went to California to see more friends and family and continue the celebrations. After all, Darryl is a wonderful part of my story and I try to celebrate him as much as possible.

When we came home from California, my 75-year-old mother-in-law, who had lived with us for 12 years, moved into her own apartment. She told Darryl and me that it was time. She needed her space and wanted to "finally" live on her own. Now, you want to talk about JOY! Not so much for us, but for Elizabeth, as she found her jam. She is lighter in her energy, she has her own tribe in the community, she cooks for people and they love her like their own grandma. She was able to let go of some of her red balloons (those things we hold on tightly to provide protection–some good balloons and others– not so much) and give herself the gift of space and being alone.

We rounded out 2018 with a huge party in October that Darryl threw for me to celebrate publishing **JOY Warrior**. By then it was time for another girls trip; mother/daughter with Maddison and me. We went to the beautiful mountains of Colorado and spent time getting to know each other again. (Free advice: you must do this with your daughters when they become women.)

warrior strong

Thanksgiving came and my family was in Kansas City for the weekend and we played "Mix Tape" every night! We went to the mall and we watched football and completed every task with family that you should do together over the holidays. December came and we were "Rockin' around the Christmas tree" for many weeks. My house was full of people and parties and it was exactly what we live for every holiday season.

In January of 2019, with my chosen word of BLOOM, I turned 50. It was EPIC! My beautiful husband gave me 50 cards and celebrations for 50 days straight (Sorry ladies, he's taken!) My final gift was something I had waited for all the years we had been together. Darryl told me to go and get the dog I always wanted. Leo Ephram Robinson, an F1 Goldendoodle, is my sun, moon and all the bright stars. He moved into the Farley house on February 13, 2019. He is JOY every day in the family by simply being in our space. He came from Corydon, Iowa, where my dear friend Angela is from, so he's an Iowa dog—Wayne County—and that is everything to me. Iowa is where I'm from and where so many of my loved ones lived and still live.

In April, our girls trip was huge. We went to Vegas to celebrate five years of being cancer free. We laughed and cried and spent time just being together. We spent too much time in the pool, with a lot of vodka and even more sun. There were days at the spa and nights with Chippendales …but I digress. I will never forget that time, or my tribe of beautiful women who were with me on that anniversary. There are too many stories and moments to share, but I can tell you for certain that Mortadella is never sold at Wal-Mart, much to Trang's complete dismay (she has a serious thing with high-end deli meats) and Danielle and Mimi voted that In & Out is the best burger they have ever had. More JOY!

My husband was honored with receiving an award for President's Club with his company. Another excuse for a trip as we were off to Torrey Pines for four days of spoiling and true first-class experiences. I am always proud of Darryl's work ethic and determination and this was a time to celebrate with many of his team members. We will never forget the friendships and memories that were made on that trip to California. We took in that time, listened to the whispers and smiled from ear to ear with the JOY we celebrated.

In June of 2019, our dear friends, the Jacksons, were on their "baseball games across America tour." They stayed with us in Kansas City. That called forth more pure JOY just to have them in our home and show off our lovely city.

In July we attended an annual pig roast at Dannielle's house. People in the family fly in for this event–it is that epic. I was wearing a cute maxi dress and it was really hot that day. Midway through the party I stood up on a chair in Danielle's dining room and my dear friend Kay cut the dress to a much shorter length. That's what my tribe is there for–always, and without question. When life gets too hot, they let the heat out. They keep me from hurting myself when running with scissors. And Mimi always makes sure to capture every single moment on camera so we can talk and laugh about it for years to come. This is why everyone needs a tribe!

We rounded out the year with so many friends, several dinner parties, and way too many holiday parties to list. I hugged my family goodbye at Christmas in Iowa. We promised to see one another again very soon. After an intimate dinner party hosted by Carla, we hugged goodbye with our sides still hurting from laughter and true JOY from the evening. We made plans for the new year and promised to get together again very soon. These were all moments I took pictures of in my mind and put away for another day, not even imagining I would not see anyone for a very long time.

Darryl and I decided, as 2019 ended, that we were blessed to have laughed and loved our way through an entire year. We were beyond excited to jump into 2020. It was going to be the year of VISION, to use a cliche´. I had selected my word for the new year, as I do at the closing of each year. For 2020 it would be FLY. But I had no idea how high, or for how long I would remain suspended without a parachute.

> *"People come into your life for a reason, a season or a lifetime. When you figure out which it is, you will know exactly what to do."*
> Brian Chalker

In February of 2020, I was working with a client in New Orleans. Darryl was with me on this work trip. I remember in the early morning hearing a news report and not paying much attention to the details, "A Chinese tourist who tested positive for the virus has died in France." I heard this and wrote about it later that day in my journal. Sadly, I thought nothing more about it, merely marking time in the journal.

There is a beautiful poem I have read many times titled, "A reason, A season and a Lifetime." New Orleans was this poem, lived out loud. I felt it at the time we were in the city, and in the days and weeks and even the year after we left. I listened to the whispers in New Orleans and felt so much energy.

We were there for only three days yet were surrounded by some of the most beautiful people. It was as if Norman Rockwell decided we needed to encounter every level of human culture possible. We ate in fantastic restaurants and stayed in a great hotel just off Bourbon Street. What struck me as unique was the age of so many of the hospitality workers. They were much older than my husband and me. Yet they had a vibe and electricity they carried deep in their souls; they were warrior strong and you could feel it. They shared stories with us at every opportunity. Many worked to put grandchildren through college or make sure their elderly parents wanted for nothing. Still more were retired officers from the military having one thing in common, and it was palpable–you felt their gratitude. They led every exchange with humility and a simple joy that was not common in the climate of 2020. And now, as I am writing my new tiny book, it seems to be escaping my vision by the day.

On March 13, 2020, one of my oldest and dearest friends, Angela, was in Kansas City with her family for March Madness. We were standing in my living room watching the television for updates to the games when suddenly, in front of us, March Madness was cancelled.

By the hour, the NBA cancelled and Broadway went dark. Disneyland was shutting down its parks (all of them), the stock markets were in a freefall. On March 16, New York City closed their schools (all of them.) My husbands' company cancelled its national sales conference for the following week and major retailers were closing their stores…just shutting the doors and sending their employees home. California issued a stay-at-home order and then New York issued a "pause" (was this stay-at-home lite?)

By March 27, the United States surpassed 100,000 cases of the novel coronavirus that we would all come to refer to as Covid, and by March 31, 2020 we (the entire country) shut down, at our homes, "sheltering in place." The virus was in the United States and it was bad.

I watched everything I could and felt as if I had an intimate relationship with Dr. Anthony Fauci and Governor Andrew Cuomo. For some reason, the words from these complete strangers kept me calm and helped me to get blindly through the madness we were living in.

I could not believe, in such a short time, how much JOY we had been a part of or how these memories would be essential to keeping me strong. I had to remember hugging my father in December of 2019. Because, as I am writing this today in May of 2021, I have yet to hug him again.

How and why did we decide to move my mother-in-law into her own space prior to the pandemic? Yet thankfully, she was in a bubble in her tiny community, safe from harm.

As for me, I had just opened myself to the world again in 2018 after being ill for so long. And now I have to quarantine? What the hell did that mean anyway? And do they have cable in Quarantine? Did I have enough in my reserve tank of life to survive another crisis?

warrior strong

I started looking for my warrior suit. It was time to get very quiet and once again listen to the whispers.

"Crisis does not build character, it reveals it!"
James Lane Allen

TAKE A MOMENT AND WRITE WHAT YOU HAVE BEEN THROUGH. WRITE ABOUT HOW STRONG YOU ARE!

_____
_____
_____
_____
_____
_____
_____
_____
_____
_____
_____
_____
_____
_____
_____
_____

2.2

Can't Change Your Past, Change Your Perspective and Then... Your Team Wins the Super Bowl!

The year 2020 began with so much to offer us: A new decade, a constant analogy to more clear vision, time to begin anew. I had toiled over my defining word for this year for almost 30 days straight. FLY was everything to me. Like JOY, it was tiny and mighty. FLY had power and possibilities, promise and direction. The opening act of this unbelievable drama was vibrant and exhilarating, especially if you lived in Kansas City!

I was 50 years old when the Kansas City Chiefs won the game that would send them to Super Bowl 50 on February 2, 2020. I knew they were going to win. We all did. You could feel an energy from that team that we had not seen in our city in a very long time.

Darryl took a client to the game where the Chiefs played the Houston Texans on a very cold day in January and I got to go along (I am very good at entertaining spouses). We sat in the stands like frozen popsicle sticks; yet you could not have told me it was 10 degrees outside. I took several moments to breathe in the energy and listen to the whispers, to scan the huge stadium we were in and to just be in the moment singing, *"Friends in Low Places"* with Garth Brooks and 70,000 of my closest friends.

We were behind 24-0 in the second quarter and then, all of a sudden, we came back to smash the Texans, 51-31. We scored a record for a post-season game, my son told me, and because Baltimore lost (you can tell how little I understand the intricacies of football). Because they had lost the previous night, we played the Tennessee Titans. And we won. Now look out baby! We are going to the Superbowl in Miami! I had felt it all season and I kept saying this would happen. And I needed the t-shirt that said 50 years, because I was 50! All I thought about the entire ride home was throwing the biggest Super Bowl party ever at our Farley house.

The year 2020 was beginning at lightning speed. I could barely contain my JOY!

The game was being played in Miami, so of course I used this as my party theme. So many friends came to the party. Some stayed the entire night, while others came and went throughout the night. My dear neighbor Sandy thought she was bringing bad luck and she went home for a while during the game. The first half of the game was a complete back and forth. But in the fourth quarter we exploded and my house went nuts–absolutely, bat-shit-crazy nuts! Neighbors came streaming into our front door, and soon we were yelling and screaming on the street.

Then, all of a sudden, Darryl yells out, "I am going to get the T-Shirts. We gotta get the merch!"

To know Darryl Edward Robinson, you must understand and appreciate that he likes (in fact, he loves) to keep his money in the bank. So, when I tell you that we cashed out at $1200 that night getting t-shirts for everyone who kept calling us on the phone, understand this was a phenomenon almost as amazing as our Super Bowl win.

I remember the pictures I took in my mind that moment in Dick's Sporting Goods as I witnessed the yelling and cheering. Complete strangers were body-to-body in the store, helping one another with t-shirts and ball cap purchases. Grown men were hugging each other for no reason and every reason, all at the same time. It was so beautiful. I collected these images in my imaginary backpack, storing them away for another day, not knowing that crowds and the hugging of strangers would soon vanish.

On Wednesday, February 5, the city played host to a beautiful Super Bowl parade in Kansas City for our champions. Our city loves a couple of things: BBQ, Baseball and the Chiefs! It was 20 degrees outside for most of the day, but you could not tell it to look at anyone's face. Again, complete strangers danced together, took random pictures with anyone they could, and hugged as many people as possible–almost as if they were collecting tokens for hugs. This only matters now, but at the time it all seemed so normal; almost expected.

We saw so many friends in that sea of people. It was hard to imagine you could run into long-time family friends, but there they were, almost as if the universe was playing a beautiful game of chess and we were the pieces on the board. It was a magical time in our city. My dear friend Trang was living with us and she was convinced they threw the parade to welcome her home, since she had not lived here since 2006. (Trang is her own band of JOY at all times!)

On the drive home from the parade I remember thinking how truly lucky I was; how blessed my family was and how calm life felt. I considered how far we had come as a blended family and how rock-solid we were. I thought about how much my health had improved and how I was truly living my best life. Every time we turned around more JOY was waiting to be discovered. (I remembered having the same feeling on 9.10.2001.)

I have often gone back in my mind to that drive home in February. There was a lot of traffic coming out of downtown. The normal 15-minute drive home took almost an hour. We were shuffling on side streets and intersections, watching strangers get out of their cars at red lights and hug other strangers until the light turned green. It was so crazy to be a part of all of this. I was present and listening to all the whispers in the universe. My memory camera was clicking away at its fastest speed, shooting images and cataloguing them for a later place, another day, another time.

My perspective of life had completely changed in so many ways, and over many days and years. I was a different person now. I led my life with JOY. I could feel it. I was taller now when I stood up in a room. I understood what my journey in life had taken me through and marveled that I had survived it with my family, my tribe and my soul completely intact. I had a "new normal" and was killin' it!

Exactly nine days later we boarded our plane to New Orleans. We did not—and could not anticipate nor imagine—that we would not fly again for 18 months. It was impossible to believe that arenas like football stadiums or concert venues would not be occupied for that same amount of time or longer.

We had invited my dad and Linda to come to Kansas City and celebrate at the parade. But because they had just returned from an overseas trip, they wanted to rest. We thought nothing of this, and knew they would be here sometime later in the month to pick up the "merch" and see what the city had transformed into since winning the Super Bowl! We were so wrong.

I did not know then that the hugs I shared with my family at Christmas of 2019 would be the last for over 16 months. We had no crystal ball to process the amount of death and absolute destruction that were in our headlights in the oncoming traffic. We were experiencing our last burst of JOY and it was going to be up to all of us to dig into our invisible backpacks and pull out what we had been collecting for most of our lives. We would soon have to go back to a time where memories and spaces could keep us calm and safe from the ensuing trauma.

A few years previously, I had accidentally become a *JOY Warrior*. I was ready for what was coming…or so I thought.

"JOY is a glimpse at the world being right."
                                               Ashley Anthis

JANUARY 1, 2020......WHAT GAVE YOU JOY?

_____
_____
_____
_____
_____
_____
_____
_____
_____
_____
_____
_____
_____
_____
_____
_____
_____
_____

2.3

Let Your Inside Light Shine Bright; It Will Glow From Your Shaved Head

In 2018 I wrote in the prologue to my first book, "I am a self-proclaimed JOY Warrior. I am a better human being for having been the only driver on this journey without a map. I made it through my trip by having faith and not dying in fear ...."

That proclamation aside, I am not going to lie. I shaved my head almost immediately when the pandemic shutdown happened. One reason was to be completely practical. Gary, my dear friend and the man who helps me to look normal, had to close down his shop. Secondly, if I was going to warrior up, I would need to channel my inner GI Jane. (I wish this would have gotten me in better shape in 2020, but that is another book in the self-help section that I will not write about…ever.

Recently we passed the one-year anniversary of our shutdown in this country and I feel like the measurement in units of time was in dog years. We lived seven years in one during 2020.

In the beginning, I got very quiet. I did not panic, but neither was I calm on the inside. I went to Costco too much. I still am going through my toilet paper and Clorox wipes and thankfully we have finally used the 150 lbs. of rice I bought in March of last year. Mind you, I was quite methodical and organized when making these purchases and decisions every day for two straight weeks. You know it's bad when everyone is wearing masks and the Costco greeter calls you by name to say hello. My husband would say I was trying to help promote the falling economy. But I know I was just in complete event planner mode. If this was an event, we needed a plan, supplies, supplies to back up the supplies, Plan D to back up plan A, B and C. It all felt so foreign and even out-of-body for many weeks into our "shelter in place" days. But I was determined to fake it to make it!

In between hours of consuming news from every media outlet possible, I went back to my roots—the beginning of the journey when I had became so sick. I went back to my health practices on a daily and weekly basis. Meditation helped me more than anything during 2020. The sauna was used weekly in our house by someone. I walked Leo every single day, rain or shine, three times a day, without fail. In fact, the poor dog is going to have a major readjustment when we all leave the house and are back to normal. In those early days I had to create a routine, and give myself daily tasks and weekly projects. There had to be a sense of normal in the chaos. I will be ready now for the next pandemic because I survived the 2020 boot camp.

Soon after supplies were purchased and all family and friends and their plans were accounted for, I began Amazon shipping of necessary supplies (again, promoting of the economy). Then I began to quietly reflect, almost daily, on what life had given to me from 2018 until now. How many unbelievable trips I had the pleasure to take in such a short amount of time! How many parties and dinners we hosted for every season and no reason at all! How much laughter and JOY was living in my invisible backpack! All those moments and memories gave me strength for this new adventure.

I reflected, with complete gratitude, that during the time we were losing my mother it was 2012/2013 and not 2020. When my health crisis began, it was 2013 and not 2020. Once the gratitude and mindful prayers were completed, I felt guilt and was riddled with overwhelming sadness for all the strangers who were going through exactly what I had endured. But now they were doing this in a pandemic—all alone—absent their tribes.

Every day I made it my mission to shine my inside light bright. This was not easy in 2020.

I looked into the eyes of strangers when I had to go to the store, smiling with my eyes now, since our smiles were covered. I moved more slowly everywhere I went and respected people's spaces and the need to stay safe in their own bubbles. I was trying every day to turn our collective pain into purpose, realizing that we cannot understand death by reading about it; it requires experience for understanding. I knew that from my own journey and was shocked as we moved deeper into 2020 that so many people were "indifferent" to the notions of compassion and empathy.

My April to-do lists told me to buy a new TV for my father, who was turning 70. This pains me to write because, of course, the perpetual event planner in me had already planned a huge party to surprise my dad in Kansas City.

My father loves two things at a party—great carrot cake and dancing to fantastic music. We had planned to do all of this and more. Instead, Darryl and I masked and gloved up and went to Best Buy. It was empty, quiet, and we were in and out in about 15 minutes. We had the new TV shipped to his front door as a surprise and a way to open a window when the world had closed the doors. With the aid of my passwords to every streaming network possible, he and Linda's world would not be so small now. They could make lists of programs to watch together. This plan would make the days not so long and the nights much calmer. This got me thinking about sending a box to them every month during the pandemic. And after 14 months of doing this, Darryl believes I am totally committed to promoting the economy at every juncture.

During this time Darryl had some blood work that came back at the end of April that did not seem right. But we brushed it aside and were both glad to be healthy and safe, free from Covid. However, the universe oversees what is written and evidently needed to shake up our 2020—like two wet cats in a paper bag.

My father turned 70 on May 1, 2020. Pam, my dear friend from high school, picked up a cake I had ordered from Hy-Vee and delivered it to his front porch. But, not only was my dad a bit fearful of everything that was going on in the world, (as we all were) he also did not make the connection that this was a young lady who had spent many nights in his house when his daughters were teenagers. When Pam told him Happy Birthday and knew his name, he was mildly freaked out. Soon after many FaceTime calls with family and friends to confirm Pam's identity, we had to jump on another call with a doctor who wanted to speak to my husband.

We had to speak with a specialist about the blood work and more tests needed to be run, but because of Covid, perhaps they could wait. Nothing much to worry about, we were told (which is the exact moment you begin to worry and Google everything under the sun. Besides, I have my MD from Google and can use it on a moment's notice.

I kept my notes that I scribbled when the doctor was talking to us on the phone: "Something did not feel right to me about your lab work. Stop the meds you are taking; they are counterproductive. Pituitary adenoma. I am sending you to a neurologist who is great at removing masses. Yours looks to be about 2.2 cm, which is significant, and it needs to come out. Nothing to worry about."

Brain tumor! Benign brain tumor! In a freakin' pandemic?

My husband, who has never had any health issues in his entire life, would have to be an overachiever (as he very often is) and have a brain tumor!

There! I've said it! Those of you appalled by my open disgust for a brain tumor...good! I hated that mass. I hated that Darryl was going through this. I hated that it was a pandemic. Then I was just MAD. I was scared and I was mad. Not a good combination for a woman who is "a self-proclaimed JOY Warrior" and so big on calm and quiet meditation. This time the circumstances were severely disrupting my chi and killing the Zen gardens I cultivated in my mind. We were on red alert!

The thing about letting JOY be your superpower is that it is a form of gratitude to share with yourself and others. The universe loves gratitude and will use this to conspire for good. Darryl had a very light and easily accessible invisible life backpack. He is the master of understanding that emotional energy is finite. Because of the way he manages his energy, he lives with a powerful reserve. He called the brain tumor his "ADVENTURE" (Yes, I agree; something was truly wrong with him!)

We did not know, going into Memorial Day weekend, but he would be our rock over the summer months. He would support a strong family foundation with a big ass tumor in his head. His warrior suit is "on" at all times. And that's what makes him our superhero.

"If your compassion does not include yourself, it is incomplete."
Buddha

DO YOU GIVE YOURSELF GRACE? HOW DID YOU DO THIS IN 2020?....

_____

_____

_____

_____

_____

_____

_____

2.4

'Separately United, We Are Alone Together.'
We've Become A Country Western Song!

On May 25, 2020 a complete stranger changed the trajectory of my summer.

A precious young man whom I had never met, called out for his mother who had died several years earlier. He was surrounded by strangers in the heat. He was alone; he was afraid. And he was murdered on a city street in America by a police officer kneeling on his neck.

In the days after the murder of George Floyd, I read a tweet from Russell Simmons. He challenged everyone to "say something." I took these words personally; almost as personally as the last words Mr. Floyd spoke—"I can't breathe."

My words are not a statement of disdain for police. I have the utmost respect for police officers. We have taught our children to have the same respectful attitudes, and they do. This is about a division that exists in our country. This is about the silence that people exercise when tragedies are made public. In the hot summer of 2020, I chose not to do that ANYmore. In the middle of a pandemic, I found my voice. I needed to be able to tell my children that I did not and would not stay silent.

Years earlier I sat with my husband at our kitchen table when he had "the talk" with DJ and Maddison about being black in America. About how exhausting it truly can be. And that having that feeling was absolutely okay. So,. what do you do with that and how do you not let it define you? He talked to them about how they needed to remain calm and sometimes even quiet when they interacted with people. They needed to be careful citizens; not wear their hoods up or play loud music when driving. They were instructed by my husband about how to "survive the encounters."

My son DJ is 6'6". He constantly needs to be careful that his presence in a room is not intimidating. Darryl explained to Maddison that women who are not black will comment on her skin tone or her hair. Many would be curious and perhaps not know or understand. Many would have something to say—especially if she someday dated a white man. Darryl always tried to end the conversations with the kids on the positive note that we are all interconnected as human beings; we are all living and breathing organisms who matter and we are all trying to figure life out, TOGETHER.

I barely slept for three days after hearing the news about the death of Mr. Floyd. I could not bring myself to watch the video. This was too close to home for me. This could have been someone in MY family. When my tears dried, I was angry. I was frustrated and I was scared. But I was also living in a world of privilege, untouched by anything this monstrous or unforgivable.

If you know me, you know that my family is my everything. They are my crew. They are my JOY and happiness (also my occasional stress and anxiety). We live in the middle of America, what many refer to as "flyover country," in Overland Park, Kansas. I love being married to my best friend Darryl and being a momma to DJ and Maddison. After George Floyd's death, I posted my family picture on social media with the caption, "the death of George Floyd matters so much...this could have been someone in my family."

It's so easy to see how it could happen. My son, at 23, has been placed on the ground and handcuffed for no reason at all. When he was in eighth grade, Darryl had to talk to DJ about running in the neighborhood and cutting through back yards after football practice. He could be arrested, or worse, shot for trespassing.

My daughter Maddison, also only 23 years young, has been shopping in a store in Alabama when a clerk would not check her out and asked the white person behind her to come through the line. This was after the clerk had followed her through the Target!

On another occasion, we received her tearful phone call when Maddison and her friend were stopped in Oklahoma in a gated community where they were going to visit a friend. They were told they "did not belong," even though they had been invited by someone living there! You cannot imagine the pain a parent had when receiving these phone calls. I felt so badly for my kids. Their life backpacks were becoming heavy.

Darryl, who fears nothing but snakes, holds a visceral fear all the time about being confronted by someone who gets outside of themselves because of the color of his skin. He is my rock and he would never show me or anyone around him that life in his world is heavy. in fact, it's an extra 100 lb. backpack he carries every day.

Following many days of thought and prayer, tears and anger, I was moved to do something. So I created **#StandOnSwitzer** as a tiny ripple that could make a difference.

For 23 weeks– every Sunday at seven–in the name of Black Lives Matter, we were strangers standing together who became friends. We supported a common goal–to love thy neighbor. All of us represented different races and religions. We told our collective stories, always listening more than we spoke. We did not fix everything in 23 weeks, but we did create an invisible door for future neighbors to walk through and feel equal. We were WOKE. We "Welcomed the Opportunity to show Kindness and Empathy." We hosted conversations, not confrontations.

Quickly into our journey I became keenly aware of the insecurity and incivility living in my own back yard. I was disappointed to find that many "neighbors" wanted nothing to do with any suggestion that Black Lives Matter. But we did not give up. Our tribe was committed, despite haggling and harassment from many passersby. A hundred strangers were not a moment. We created a Middle America movement, and it was beautiful. I took this in and engraved it in my soul...all the faces, all the stories we shared. We are forever interconnected now, because what we did mattered and that was and is real JOY.

Our divisions with one another will begin to change with conversations. Speaking together in back yards, or at simple neighborhood potluck dinners together, we can plant community gardens for the future, where seeds of equality grow, and nourish the souls of everyone living together. This is what makes me PROUD! Kindness and JOY should be how we lead every conversation. While understanding that people don't know what they don't know, it's the responsibility of all of us to begin conversations. Or, as Russell Simmons challenged us all, "Say something".

"We cannot force someone to hear a message they are not ready to receive, but we must never underestimate the power of planting a seed."

My husband explains racism in such a non-confrontational way. This is why he's our North Star. Darryl has said that we ALL begin our lives with a five-burner stove. We have the ability to produce heat, make things possible, share with others, create moments….all similar to what a five-burner stove can do for a family.

Some people have five burners, and they can access these at any time. This is a privilege. Some people have five burners and they only need to access two or three at a time in order to make their "kitchen table of life" successful. But if you are poor, you have to give up one of your burners, because a lot of time is spent trying to get out of that situation. If you are poor and black, now you have to give up two of your burners, because so much time is spent managing both these parts of your life. It can be exhausting. Now you are left with three burners, which could be great, but you have to go through your life and live, so now you are down to only two. What happens if your remaining two get damaged or they stop working, and you have no backup. You are out of burners. Yet there are many people in this world (like me) who never have to use all their burners, and who would not even consider it.

Every time Darryl gives this analogy, tears well up in my eyes. This is deeply emotional and something I cannot stop.

Racism, quite simply, is a hatred or fear of what we do not understand about others. But OPEN conversations are the catalysts to put change into action. One day at a time, one person and situation at a time, I try to share my extra burners with someone who does not have as many available. This is how we all can create a movement; not just live in moments. We became separate and united. We were alone in our homes and yet, as a nation, many of us came together. We were a freakin country western song!

As hard as the summer of 2020 was–and the months following were not much better–I still had an attitude of gratitude with everything I was a part of.

"Gratitude turns all that we have into enough."

This anonymous quote is very powerful and gives perspective to why I write about such a heavy subject in this tiny little book. JOY to me means "just open yourself." It is an understanding that we all have something in common, because we all have something to be thankful and grateful for. Gratitude makes what we have in our life enough. When we decide to take a "moment" to have a conversation, and allow this to be awkward and even uncomfortable, we will find a space of calm where we can listen to the whispers and hear...

"Tomorrow belongs to the people who prepare for it today."
African Proverb

"Daddy changed the world!"

Gianna Floyd

MEMORIAL DAY WEEKEND 2020, WE SHELTERED IN PLACE.
MAY 26 WE CAME OUT OF OUR HOMES AND MARCHED....

Did you participate in any marches in 2020? Judgement free, why or why not?

How did you speak with your family about what was happening?

If you could go back in time, what would you do differently?

2.5

Plant Seeds of Hope, Ground Yourself, Then Water with Gin & Tonic

June of 2020 began in the same manner as my old life as a high-end events designer. I had the illusion of calm because I am always organized. But just under the surface, buried in the color-coded schedule, lies complete and utter chaos.

We had a phone call with Darryl's doctor, who told us that his brain tumor needed to come out sooner rather than later because it was pressing on his optic nerve. It would be bad if he woke up one morning blind. Picture my reaction–a cartoon bubble full of expletives.

Following many phone calls and appointment scheduling, added to the dance around Covid with several healthcare professionals, we had a date for the surgery–September 8. Finally we have what I live for–A PLAN! However, it was mid-June and how in the hell was I going to get to September 8 with my sanity intact?

Gin and tonic for breakfast everyday? We were in a pandemic, so who would know? Seriously...is this the solution?

Something many know about me, (and it's sad to admit, but it's who I am, and I just have to embrace that) is that I major in minor events. What do you do when life is crazy and chaotic? I just add more heat. I needed to find happiness for the next couple of months. Just one tiny problem with finding happiness in the chaos. Just a little thing called a pandemic. I can't go anywhere or visit anyone. I can't be in the ocean, where the water talks to me and calms my soul. So, instead I listen and pay attention to the whispers in my life. I have fine-tuned my ability to be ever present in many things and life then hands me an opportunity for just such a moment–a burst of JOY!

My nieces, Sophia and Elizabeth, who were 11 at the time, were coming to Kansas to visit my mother-in-law the first week of July. They missed Grandma terribly, as she did them, and because of the pandemic it had been way too long since they were all together. The girls lived in a quarantine bubble before traveling to Kansas City with my brother and sister-in-law. They arrived just before their 12th birthday anniversaries. It was a wonderful time for us. We had family in town again, and for a moment, life was "normal."

The girls were supposed to start online school in August, but some wires (or emails) got crossed. Suddenly, they needed to go to online school in two days. Yep, cue the music–Crazy Town is on full display. And this is where I come in, as the conductor of crazy.

I love moments like this; I embrace them. I went into full-on teacher mode. I set up a school in the dining room, created schedules and lists, learned about zoom calls and their homework lessons on Canvas. My friend, Trang, who was still living at The Farley House, made them gourmet lunches every day. After all, what else were we doing with our time during a pandemic?

The girls played soccer in the backyard with Leo after every lunch, and we had dinner at night on the patio for ten weeks. I know this time was helpful to my sister-in-law, Michelle, and she shared her gratitude constantly with Darryl and me. What the tiny humans did not know is that they gave us so much more. They helped me keep my warrior suit intact; even shined it up a bit. In chaos, we all can create calm and JOY. We just have to look for moments and understand they are opportunities–what I lovingly refer to as joyful bursts.

Another time capsule of joy for us in the summer of 2020 was a space at Table Rock Lake owned by my dear tribe members, Crystal and Michelle. We went to the lake in June and August. Even at the time, I knew how much these moments were leaving a handprint on my soul.

Our first trip to TRL was in June, right before the twins arrived. We loaded the truck with Trang and enough food to keep a small village alive for a month. We were only going for three days, but this is life and cooking with Trang. We were on Crystal's boat every day and soaked up the sunshine. We laughed and cried a bit and just lived in the bubble of "normal" we created. We played Polish Poker, which has so many instructions you have to follow a framed list. This proved challenging to me while simultaneously drinking cocktails and holding conversations at a pace that would give U.N. interpreters a run for their money.

We went back to the lake in August. My friend Danielle and Trang went along. This trip was different. Darryl had warned me that he did not want anyone at the lake to know about the brain tumor.

"Let's just get away–not have it be the topic of conversation all weekend," he said. I reluctantly agreed to the limits on our conversations, but only because I love my husband so much. On the inside I was screaming mad, unable to sleep well, scared to death and pacing the hallways at night while Darryl was sleeping. But then calm came over me and I reminded myself that Darryl was the patient, not me. Over and over, I repeated these words to the ceiling, where I talk when I am having a conversation with God–"It's not about me!"

That second weekend at the lake was even better than the first trip, which was hard to top. Because on both trips Crystal made "lake bacon." I can't share anything more on this. If you don't get invited, you can't know the marvel of this bacon. Crystal and Michelle hosted Gary, Danielle, Trang, Darryl, and me. There was so much laughter and friendship, games, relaxation, more games, more laughter and true love among most dear friends. Then Crystal said to us on Saturday night, "Let's go out in the morning and go on a sunrise cruise. I don't always do this, but we should tomorrow." We agreed.

In the morning Darryl was tired and did not go. I was now worried. I would be alone with my tribe. This should be my moment to scream out what was about to happen and what we had been going through all summer long.

I did not understand how my warrior suit would be needed that weekend. I didn't even know it was waterproof. But there it was ready and accessible and able to keep me strong.

As the boat rounded a cove that morning we saw the most beautiful sunrise coming over the horizon—with brilliant colors of sapphire and tangerine—and with music playing from Crystal's playlist. And I just wept. Only recently did Crystal understand that I was not crying from the beauty of that sunrise but because I was so afraid of losing my husband in the surgery. I could not begin to even conceive not having his energy in my orbit. You see, he is my sun. How would I find JOY if his light went out?

We were on the boat for about an hour and just as we were about to come into the slip, I felt a deep exhale and then warmth. I felt a calm around me that seemed to say, "It's going to be okay, friend. How are you going to respond to this season? Let your response be what you fix your gaze upon."

I walked back into the house and Darryl was there waiting for us. I hugged him tighter than I think I have ever done before. He asked me if I was okay. I smiled, teared up again and went downstairs to be alone, to take a moment just to breathe and take in what had just happened to me.

I had been so connected with the universe in those 60 minutes that I still tear up today just typing these words on my computer. I did not run from this feeling. I understood and was totally aware this was JOY, even though I was crying. If this past year and my journey up to this point has taught me anything, it has underscored that you cannot change what is already written. If it is time to clock out and go to the big dance in heaven, no playlist or mixtape I put together… no spectacular celebration or party… will stop this from happening.

I did not need to major in minor events before Darryl went into his surgery. I needed to have faith, pray, believe, pray some more and rest. I needed to understand that this moment was not about me or my children. It was only about Darryl, and he was not worried. We should not be either. I was now ready to embrace "the adventure."

We left Table Rock Lake that day and I felt different about that beautiful space than I ever had before. It was a place where delicate spirits live and breathe. Not just anyone can attend; it is sacred. That weekend at the lake was our church–a space to pray and be with our feelings separately and individually. Our present troubles are quite small, and perhaps what we cannot see could last forever. We needed to accept where we all were at that moment and listen to the whispers.

I was given strength on that weekend to be a rock for my husband. He was–and is–always my priority, but my position was wrong. I needed to pull back and accept that I was not driving this boat.

The clouds and the waters we saw and felt that weekend... they held the power. The spirit of beautiful Mother Earth held the healing and the grounding we needed, and everything was going to be okay.

My husband went into surgery on Tuesday, September 8 at 6:10 a.m. and was out in ICU at 12:47 pm. His surgery was a complete success. If you saw him today, you wouldn't be able to tell that he is a brain surgery survivor; a warrior with not even the hint of a "bad ass" scar. They went in through his nasal cavity and took out the tumor.

Science and technology are truly amazing. The steady hands and gifts of the doctor's experience and know-how are almost unbelievable. Darryl is fully recovered and stronger than ever, just as it was meant to be.

Our dear friends (whom we lovingly refer to as "The Family

Stone") helped us every day through this most difficult time and we are forever grateful. Their tribe, led by Charlotte, called daily and sometimes hourly, just checking in. They had Amazon packages at the door and did anything they could to lighten the load. Robert Stone and Darryl had played basketball together in college; they are "hand-picked brothers." The Stones are our family and this big ugly mass of a tumor made us feel like we lived in the same house for a moment in time. And suddenly, there it was again–JOY!

When I wrote **JOY Warrior**, I spoke at length about the need for a tribe. I needed these people in order to survive my own storm and now they keep me strong. Their net is wide, and I am lifetime-blessed that they always keep me steady. They are the reasons I made it to my new tomorrows. I invite everyone reading my tiny little book to open up and list your tribe. It's not about quantity; it's quality. Notice the people who make an effort to stay in your life through the worst of times. This, my friend, is your tribe.

The summer of 2020 taught me to plant seeds of hope. I had to tend to these growing seeds daily. I had to nourish them with equal parts of sunshine and water. That summer I learned that the parent of all emotions in my life is GRATITUDE. From this come the children called JOY, EMPATHY, KINDNESS AND LOVE. These beautiful emotions have many siblings. Some are PEACE, GRACE and, most of all–HOPE.

We were living in a time where hope was scarce and difficult to locate. We had to warrior up and plant our own seeds and cultivate them. Sometimes life is going to be that way. We are going to encounter a situation–or many situations–that cause us to light the five-burner stove and survive. How much nicer our journey can be if we have planted seeds along the way to cultivate and help us bloom. These seeds become flowers to decorate our family tables and provide not only color and beauty, but also calm and that most important connection to Mother Earth. This grounds us in a space where we can listen to the whispers and find the JOYs just waiting to be discovered.

"The perceptual tendency to fill in the gaps in order to perceive disconnected parts as whole objects is called closure."
— Psychology 101

HAVE YOU MADE CLOSURE WITH 2020? HOW?

_____

_____

_____

_____

_____

_____

_____

2.6

While going through a spiritual expedition, can you earn mileage?

I am truly a blessed woman; one who rents a space in our beautiful world and who is surrounded by adults older and wiser than I. Two of these people happen to be my dear friend Lionel's parents.

You have to understand the many layers of my tribe. My girl band–Danielle, MiMi and Michelle–are sisters who make up part of my tribe. Michelle is married to a wonderful man named Lionel. His parents, Mr. and Mrs. Colon, are everything to their family and to all who are lucky enough to be "adopted" by them.

Mrs. Colon had Covid. She told me that during her time in the hospital she felt heavy, like she needed to clear the "weight around her." Her need was music to my ears, since I love to help people declutter their spaces. (What can I say–it's another level of event planning.) I delight in taking what you have, choosing what gives you JOY (thank you, Marie Kondo) and getting rid of the rest. I love moving things around, adding or subtracting color to your house's palette, and voila! New you–new view!

I stopped by the Colon's for a visit at the end of September, when Darryl was home and I was able to leave the house for a couple of hours a day while he was resting. Mrs. Colon (whom we all call Mommy) told me about her thoughts and prayers while she was sick...how she felt on the inside about what she was going through, but also what she felt about her family and the beautiful life she had lived. Mommy is one of the most faithful and spiritual people I have ever encountered. She believes, to her soul's core, that we are all beautiful people who deserve happiness and love. You feel this in her presence every time you are around her. Her face lights up with JOY, whether she sees you for the first time or the 50th time. It's always pure and from a place and a space of love.

Her wonderful husband, whom everyone calls Pops, is a strong Puerto Rican who served in the Air Force and then was a police officer for many years. He and Mommy raised their two sons and now have two grandsons that their world orbits around. Pops tries to jog almost every day and Mommy's purpose is to take care of everyone else. This makes her happy; this is her JOY.

I came into her space by invitation to help "lighten" the load. We decluttered, and the family helped to repaint many walls. We decluttered some more and moved things around, opened spaces up, let in the light. When our time together was over, she told me repeatedly how happy she was…how she felt lighter and how she needed this so badly. She was forever grateful.

I love Mommy and Pops dearly and always tell her sons how grateful I am that they loan their love out to me. My time with Mrs. Colon gave me something much more than I gave to her. I was able to go into my heart and get very quiet for many weeks. I had been Warrior Strong since March in my living room with Angela. I was fighting with everything I had to keep us safe and I was so tired. There was a pandemic outside our walls, and inside we had a tumor. I felt on many levels that I was backsliding from all the progress I had made in my journey to become a strong JOY Warrior.

But in the quiet of sorting and cleaning and sorting some more for Mommy and Pops, I reminded myself how far I had come before 2020. I went back in memory to the crazy ride that was 2018 and 2019, and knew once again why I love to go through life collecting moments and memories in my invisible backpack. What is going to happen in life is most certainly already written. This is why I collect things. I don't know when I will have to call upon what I saved; seeing beauty, happiness, healthy smiles and JOY. If you are not living in a present state of calm, you must infuse calm into the chaos in the same way you put lavender bath salts in a tub of hot water. They settle the heat so that all you feel as you sink into the moment is safe, relaxed, and Warrior Strong.

warrior strong

    I found something in 2020 that I was not looking for. My strong warrior suit gave me insulation and a space to be okay with becoming another "new" version of myself. I found my true voice and used this to speak out loud to a crowd about what was wrong and what was right. I stood in my own truth and didn't care what others thought. I defended those who were defenseless and spoke out against hate. This took courage and strength. Now I am moving vertically in my life. I feel powerful on the inside and this assures me that the broken world outside my doors cannot cause me harm.

    Throughout the entire year that we all survived and lived through, friends kept asking me if I was "freaked out" or "worried" about getting sick. I would be lying if I said I was not worried. Of course I was. We all were. What we experienced during this time as a people, a human race, was indescribable loss. This is something history will record as it has in the past. Just as history includes the stories our parents and grandparents used to tell us about where they were and what was going on when they were younger, and how their lives were forever changed.

    This time we all spent together in 2020 will be so much more significant to history than anything we have ever witnessed before. However, I fear the damage to people's spirits and beliefs about what is right and wrong has shifted and it will take years to reset. What I am most positive about, and what I am sitting in my office recording as fast as I can type, is that I am certain we each control our own happiness. We can choose to infuse the JOY and we MUST learn to be grateful and actively practice gratitude. This is the secret sauce.

    In cooking there is something my friends have taught me (since I don't really cook). It's called the "holy trinity." As a young Catholic girl, I would have giggled out loud in Mass if someone had said this to me about cooking. I grew up knowing the holy trinity to be something very different.

When you cook, if you combine onion, celery, and carrots on low and slow in olive oil, the combined flavors form a base that can be used in many dishes.

Extending the metaphor a bit, we as people are this secret sauce; or at least we should be. Some of us are onions. Onions are loaded with antioxidants, which are very good for us. They contain cancer-fighting compounds. They control blood sugar and help with digestion. However, onions can also make you tear up and begin crying with the insert of the knife blade into its many complex layers.

Celery is also rich in vitamins and minerals; most importantly– vitamins A, C and K. It is low in sodium and high in potassium and balances out blood sugar. But celery can get caught very easily in your teeth, which makes eating it a bit tricky.

Finally we have carrots, the warriors of veggies for the body. Carrots are rich in beta carotene that the body changes into vitamin A, keeping our eyes strong and healthy. Carrots are classified as a superfood. When Maddison was little, I wanted to do everything possible to make sure her eyes were strong and protected, so I fed her carrots every day. She became a bit orange and my pediatrician advised me to slow down a bit.

I went through this entire outline of the "secret sauce" to say that in the quiet time at the Colons' home, I learned that WE the collective–WE as human beings, are this holy trinity in life.

I spent most of 2020 on a spiritual expedition. (I really need to investigate whether I can collect mileage–or at least life points–for my deep dive inside.) On this journey in my strong warrior suit, I understood–in a very deep and cathartic way–we are all one. Some of us are onions, many are celery, even more are carrots; but collectively we make a base for many other things that get put on our life's five burner stove. Imagine how much we could take on and fight against if only we could be united… collectively deciding to view ourselves as ingredients in the recipe of life…

all of us individual pieces and parts, but never the whole in and of ourselves.

   Mrs. Colon loves to make beans and rice in her tiny kitchen and feed anyone she can at her beautiful table. She likes to look into people's eyes and have conversations full of laughter and love…without cell phones or distractions. She just enjoys making moments and memories. I am forever grateful she helped to give me such a spiritual recipe when I needed it most. I am proud of myself for being open enough to receive this gift and let it rest on my soul. As a result, I am stronger and more sure of who I am going to be with every passing day.

   "Let your prayers each day be about his presence, not your problems."

Rose Colon

SPIRITUAL MOMENT, PEN TO PAPER–SHARE YOUR GRATITUDE

_____

_____

_____

_____

_____

_____

_____

_____

warrior strong

2.7

Giving Is Not Seasonal. Neither Is Toilet Paper

There would be no way to describe what 2020 was without dipping my feet into the pool of politics. If you do not feel comfortable with this conversation, I really don't care (see that voice I found?) This conversation must occur because what happened in 2020 WAS FREAKING UNBELIEVABLE!

There! I got that out and now I can have a calm dialogue with you, assuming you did not throw away my tiny book.

Hear me out. Since 2016, while I was getting my life back and working at the middle school and just trying to paddle water, I watched the circus come to town and it was WILD!

Don't get me wrong. I have voted for both parties and could or might do that again. That is not what this chapter is about. This is about how people lost their collective minds and sold their souls out in the "name of one." I don't care who that "one" might be, but this is dangerous in a democracy.

I am not a political science major, a talking head or a part time correspondent for any news network (however I do have a serious crush on both Rachel Maddow and Steve Kornacki, but that is another book on another day.) However, I am the oldest daughter of a social studies teacher of 43 years. He taught me that elections and voting have consequences, and that our democracy is fragile. America is based on an idea. In 2020 we should have practiced a "loud quiet," because most communication that year was on steroids. I am sure we don't have the life bandwidth to sustain that.

Remember the five-burner stove and the holy trinity that we are all going to use to make something wonderful to eat around our collective kitchen tables? Well in 2020 this pot boiled over and some warrior suits were misguided and misused in many places. People lost their North Star and forgot that life is about gratitude and putting JOY into their beautiful backpacks to be shared with our families and complete strangers. We do this to give witness to our existence in this world, as if to say, "Here I am, I was here, I matter and I am enough." We are not meant to spew hate and spin things to get people on our side in the adult version of the most schizophrenic dodgeball game I have ever seen.

We forgot to begin each day with an attitude of gratitude or to remind ourselves that giving to one another is not seasonal. Many of us began to act like the worst version of a Black Friday run on toilet paper. It was sheer madness. But then I have to remember that we did not get here in one day and cannot be fixed quickly. Families have been broken into unrepairable pieces because of politics and that is not only unfortunate, but desperately sad, unnecessary and frightening. I want to scream out to so many, "You are losing time!"

In my humble opinion, when each of us goes through our own journey we gain a warrior suit. This suit is like a superhero suit; it is supposed to be used for good. It is referred to as a warrior suit because it is indestructible and strong, resilient and impermeable, just like the person wearing it. It is not a weapon or a piece of armor for battle. We are too fragile as human beings for that.

Hate is not something you can throw around without damaging the collective whole. We all have to watch and understand the words we speak. The power of the tongue is so strong; the seeds you plant in your garden cannot be nourished with anger and pain. That will not bring you happiness and JOY. In my short, 52-year journey I have learned and I live by a couple of things that are my truth. This helps me to find my way when a storm hits:

- *Our values become our bosses, not a person.*

- *Life is like a jigsaw puzzle. The border is our values and the inside is all the pieces and parts of our journey. The puzzle can only be put together in an efficient way if we first complete the border.*

- **Excellence is not perfection. Perfection is destructive because it is rooted in fear.**

- **Comparison is the thief of JOY**

- **Show me your friends and I will show you your future.**

I have written this before and I reminded myself again in 2020: When going on a long journey you need several things–a fight song, a map, a mantra and a tribe.

Your fight song is a personal anthem or anthems to get you through the rough moments or days. There were many songs I gravitated to in this past year of being Warrior Strong, but my three favorite songs, which I will lend to you for your own use, included:

Pink, "A Million Dreams"

Why? It kept me calm and in a happy place with the tumor. Darryl is the person my soul was meant to love, and this song underscored that for me. "Through the dark, through the door, through where no one's been before, but it feels like home."

Kim Sheehy, "Both Sides Now"
(a remake of the Joni Mitchell song)

Why? Covid and everything about 2020 had two sides. When we are children, we see the world one way, through the eyes of innocence. That can wither with age, but we have to protect innocence, even as we grow, so we can tap into this during life's storms.

Jennifer Nettles, "Thank You"

Why? The sunrise cruise, church on the lake; "...for all your kindness I am blessed." This song and its beautiful lyrics kept me warm and made me feel protected and safe.

My tribe was completely intact and my family was wonderful, but no one–absolutely no one–had a Covid map. And how can we survive on a journey with no map?

Wait! I know the answer to this question. I have been here before. *We survive because we know where we're going. And we survive when we remember where we've been.*

Many of us had our eyes closed in 2020. Our faces were covered by a mask and our hands felt tied behind our backs. Lashing out on social media or at our families about politics may have given us a sense of control and power. But that wasn't healthy because many of us strayed from the lessons we learned in kindergarten…play nice with others, tell the truth, share, don't hurt your friends, use kind words, respect one another and listen when others talk. This elementary map is what we all should instinctively follow, because it will lead us home.

Our journeys became scattered and chaotic in 2020, and JOY became political. Truth was decaying by the day and we were all so scared. Divisions among people were more evident than ever before and it meant that we were not looking at our fellow man or woman as a brother or a sister, but rather as "US vs. THEM." Tribalism became our standard operating system.

In the chaos of 2020 I found my voice and worked very every day to keep our family journey and map intact. I try to remain open to conversations and communications with others that may perhaps be difficult, but should not be ignored. We cannot fear change or a "new normal" or movement in another direction. If I had done that in 2013, I would have driven my car into oncoming traffic and would not be here today. I would have given in and given up.

Sometimes in life there is no map and you just have to play the music louder and drive until you can find a spot to pull over, ask directions and keep going forward until you reach a destination. If we cannot do this together, as a holy trinity of a people, we are never going to be in a space open enough to make a good base to cook on our five burner stoves. Instead, we will explode. I, for one, have traveled too far and worked too damn hard at becoming who I am–perfectly imperfect–and I am going to be really pissed off if we turn on ourselves and/or each other. We don't get refunds or returns on time. It just keeps marching forward.

My buddy Sean had the best advice I have ever heard. It can apply to anyone, anywhere, no matter your political beliefs, race, or religion. Sean would always tell me, in his beautiful way, "It's not nice to be not nice." I said it before and I will continue to say it out loud, to anyone who will listen, "WE ALL NEED TO BE MORE LIKE SEAN!"

Perhaps one thing we can all agree on is that 2020 was not a journey, but rather a pilgrimage…a walk into the unknown. It was a place to search for new and expanded meaning about ourselves and our relationships with others. It was a time to evaluate what truly has meaning and what weighs us down. The excess must be removed. A pilgrimage like we all made in 2020 can lead us into personal transformation, and into using calm as a superpower. When we finally are in touch with what truly matters, each of us can then go home, take a place at our respective tables and begin anew. Cue Louis Armstrong…

"What a wonderful world that would be…"

"The best journeys answer questions that, in the beginning, you did not even think to ask"

WHAT HAPPENED TO YOU ON YOUR 2020 PILGRIMAGE?

_____
_____
_____
_____
_____
_____
_____
_____
_____

2.8

How Do I Listen To The Whispers...Is That Stored In My iCloud?

When I began my journey of becoming a JOY Warrior in 2013, I had absolutely no idea how to "listen to whispers" in the universe. I laughed, truly laughed out loud, when my mother gave me that advice shortly before she died. It took time to get comfortable with the idea of simply being quiet and in a space where I could be so in tune with myself that I could actually hear words being spoken to me.

I know when you read this you might have just spit out your glass of wine (if it's red .... get seltzer water asap!) Stay with me a moment, as I am going to share something with you as a gift to put into your invisible life backpack.

Going into 2020, it was just another year. For the first moment of that new year there were still people being born, people dying, people laughing and crying. As humans we all have an energy that is put into the spaces we occupy. So, what if we were to shift the way we looked at 2020–even my tiny journey I have shared with you? What if we flip everything that we all experienced on its head and look at it from another perspective? Would that make the year more tolerable; more understandable?

Are you still with me? People stayed home with their families in 2020 for the first time (perhaps ever). They cooked meals at home. They bought board games (Amazon increased the prices of puzzles by 50% in one day!) Church congregations, synagogues and mosques got creative and prayed with their people online, together. We crowded around the television to watch "The Last Dance," the story of Michael Jordan. Would we have all done this together in any other year?

Kids made teddy bears and put them in windows and people stood together all around the world to cheer for healthcare workers every night for months and months. They just stood outside hospitals clapping for complete strangers.

What if, in looking at everything that happened to us, we shift from a microscope to a telescope, and begin looking up instead of down? I understand that sometimes answers are in the granular details, but that is also where the pain and suffering lives. But in the beautiful sky and heavens above us lives hope, opportunity, empathy, JOY! What if this seven-year dog era of 2020 was meant to shift our focus in the world–to realign what really matters and give us perspective–the exact vision that "20/20" affords us when we look with the eyes of our souls.

I do not say any of this lightly. This was a year of tremendous loss and suffering. More than 600,000 people have died in this country and, according to the Johns Hopkins dashboard on 5.25.21, more than 3,480,781 people have died in the world. These are our brothers and sisters. They all had families and people who loved them and now people who grieve for their loss. They leave an empty void into which JOY needs to flow as the filler. This is where the energy givers live.

My dear tribe member Trang lived with us for the entire year of 2020. Her job changed and she came in January, not knowing Covid was on the horizon or that her industry, the world of museums, would close down. I learned a lot about life through the eyes of Trang. Those of you who know me know that there are always many stories that go with Trang (we call this the Dao of Trang, but once again, that's another book entirely).

Trang has been my dear friend for 20 years. I met her in October of 2001 when we were both working at The Nelson-Atkins Museum of Art. She is quite an interesting character. The best thing about Trang–the absolute best thing–is that she can make you feel so happy by just being in her orbit. She is always happy herself; never stressed about anything except what's for dinner and when the discounts days are at thrift stores (this can send her into a tizzy).

During 2020, Trang lived upstairs at the Farley House in Grandma's old room. Frankly, it was nice to have someone else in the house. Besides, her fried rice and pad thai are to die for (hence the need for the GI diet when I had to warrior up!) During this most contentious year, I would talk to Trang about what was going on in the world. Most of the time she would put her hand up and stop me, or take an immediate left turn in the conversation. Finally, after a couple of derailed conversations, I asked her what was going on. Why couldn't we not talk about anything? And why was she watching Korean soap operas all day? (No joke; this really happened from January to August!)

She looked directly into my eyes and I saw her own eyes well up with tears. Calmly she said, "I cannot let it all in; it's just too much." Then she went back to eating her dinner.

I let this rest on me for a couple of days and then circled back around with her, not understanding which part of it was too much. I had endless questions to ask her. How could you possibly put up a shield around yourself and act as though nothing was happening? Isn't this denial at its finest?

Trang and I really get one another. We don't fight, but there are moments when we get a bit tense with each other, in a healthy way. (Remember, you have to be with people who help you to let out the heat.) After my long and convoluted questions, she looked at me again and said, "I won't talk about all of this crap all the time. I can't. I like the bubble I put myself in. It's my force field and you don't have to like it, but it works for me." And with that, upstairs she went.

You may be saying right now that this is a nice story and all, but what the hell does this have to do with listening to the whispers? Okay, I promise, we are almost there! Trang was a genius. And I don't say that lightly. Of course, we all need a force field. This is what gives warriors their strength; this ability to control what gets let in and what does not. The mechanism constantly decides between chaos and calm. If we remain in control of this, like the

Wizard did in OZ, we are the energy givers. We decide what to give oxygen to and what to put out and cast aside.

I immediately adopted Trang's force field and modified it to work for me in my space (new colors of course, and re-organized, etc.) My warrior-strong force field helped me through the summer of 2020. I would often use what psychologists refer to as "open posture. I call it my Superman Pose. I stand strong, with my limbs spread out and take up more space than whatever I am facing. I lean into what is coming towards me, understanding that we have to conserve our energy and only give space to what really matters.

When my mother-in-law was understandably scared and quite negative before Darryl's surgery, I quickly moved the conversation to something much lighter and calmer. I gave no oxygen to the negative. I needed our space to be open to hear the whispers, even if they were coming from the iCloud space I pay extra for every single month!

The week before Darryl's surgery, I watched the force field method on full display. Trang had decided that Darryl, because he was having surgery, would need a lot of bone broth to heal his body from the inside out. We would need a refrigerator stocked high with food so that no one had to cook.

My nieces boarded a plane home the Thursday before Darryl's surgery. On Friday, Trang woke up in full-on event mode. We were all going on an adventure and we needed to be prepared for anything. She cooked and cleaned and cooked some more–for three days. It just looked exhausting to me. But I don't think I have ever seen Trang happier.

Because I am so connected to energy, and I have learned how to take time and make time for quiet, I was able to see something beautiful happen in my own home. I did nothing. I didn't plan anything. It just happened organically, and it was beautiful. When you sit back during times of crisis and chaos, and get very quiet, there is a beauty you can see and tune into, if you can be patient.

I watched Trang toil for days over the right recipe for the bone broth. The fried rice had to have more healing ingredients for Darryl when he came home.

She was literally using the five burners on our stove, and the holy trinity of onion, celery and carrots was a part of everything she produced. The old me would have been very anxious and angry at the universe during this time before the surgery. I would have wanted to control everything in every way, making myself exhausted and useless. I did not handle this "adventure" in that way.

At the end of the "Trang cooking bonanza" there were jars of bone broth and sliced and diced healing superfoods in the refrigerator. When we left to go to the hospital on Tuesday morning at 5:30 am, we closed the door, and got into the car. I say all this only to underscore the fact that sometimes we create chaos to distract ourselves from the crazy. This used to be my "go-to" behavior, but I happily got rid of it. My force field will not allow chaos and crazy at the same time. Because in the past, I've found that too much fun at a party creates memories you cannot share on Facebook.

I understand that we humans think we always need to have more: More data, more information, 24 hours, Amazon Prime within an hour. But we are not designed to keep this pace up indefinitely. This is what causes chaos and fear and can quickly remove faith. We are meant to rest and recover and to sit quietly, alone; just to be with what we are dealing with and not always having the answers. It is in the quiet that the answers can be revealed. Then calm will come over us like a warm blanket on a fall night with the windows open.

When I am quiet in my mind (and this took time for me to learn)... when I make time and take time to just be; this is when I am most comfortable and connected to the energy in the universe. This is when I am whispered to. Like that beautiful August morning coming in after watching the sunrise on Table Rock Lake, when the whispers said, "It's going to be okay, friend. How are you going to respond to this season? Let your response be what you fix your gaze upon."

My force field was open. I was ready to accept whatever came. Call it faith, prayer, karma, peace, zen, whatever you want to call it in your own space, with your own self. I just encourage you to BE OPEN, because I am now. And I have Trang, my lovely Vietnamese friend and a member of my tribe, to thank for that!

"To know even one life has breathed easier because you have lived. This is to have succeeded."
Ralph Waldo Emerson

WILL YOU ADOPT A "FORCE FIELD" PRACTICE AND STAND IN YOUR SUPERMAN POSE?

_____

_____

_____

_____

_____

_____

_____

_____

2.9

I am OPEN; I Can See Farther Than My Eyes Can Look!

When you go through something difficult, or survive a traumatic event, the body needs time to heal. It is imperative to give yourself the gift of quiet and time. We could not, as a nation or world, do that when 2021 rolled into town. There were three Wednesdays that began in January in America that we all had to go through— Insurrection, impeachment and Inauguration.

I was exhausted and felt that I did not have any more to give. I had warriored up in 2020. I stayed strong in my family and tried as best I could to survive the storm… to find JOY in as many moments as I could and infuse laughter and light into everyday spaces to keep us balanced and warm. I had remembered to lead each day with an attitude of gratitude and patience. And the universe gave me a gift to keep moving in a forward direction, despite the ever-evolving chaos.

January 28 is my birthday. Inside my birthday card Maddison put a note that read I AM OPEN. I thought this was a great mantra since my new word for 2021 was "Becoming." I had been accepted to K-State in December and had started going back to school on January 6 to become a special education teacher. I wanted to work with as many tiny humans like Sean as I possibly could. I did not understand or appreciate the deeper meaning of the notecard on my birthday until February 6. On this day my daughter and her soon-to-be-fiancé told us they were having a baby and we were going to become grandparents. There it was, just waiting to happen! JOY. Pure and absolute JOY, living out loud in our home!

Truth be told, when they first told me and my husband, I was in shock and disbelief. I did not know what to say and I could not find words to speak. But with all I have discovered in all my life challenges, it was time to let calm run through my mind and just breathe.

I decided to just take in the moment, look at the JOY in everyone's face and be ever-present with the information. The words will come to you and then you can speak. The news just kept getting bigger and better.

In early April we had a gender reveal celebration and found out we are going to have a SONshine baby. Maddison and Ismail are having a boy! We are not only gaining another son, but a grandson!! (Insert the burst of complete JOY music here!)

I waited a long time to sit down and write another tiny book. *JOY Warrior* was the story of what I survived when I became half of my whole. The year of 2020 gave me perspective to share some more stories about how, when you become whole, you need to remain *Warrior Strong.* We have all learned only one thing this year, and that is the fragility of time. Time truly is precious. and moments and memories are always waiting to be enjoyed and the blessed are able to give them. This was a year of tremendous pain and heartache, but also of personal gains and triumphs.

I managed to avoid Covid, even with my compromised immune system, and for that I am truly grateful. Angela, one of my oldest friends, had a terrible time with this virus and is still trying to heal. Our dear friend Larry also had an awful time with Covid but is now much improved. My dad's wife, Linda, lost her father, and you can still see the pain and anger she has about Covid. There are so many stories–of so many people and so many lives–and the loss goes on and on. My heart breaks for each and every one of these families. They all had moments and memories and invisible backpacks of stories and ideas waiting to be shared, and so much JOY left unopened.

Webster's dictionary defines JOY as "a condition or feeling of high pleasure or delight; happiness or gladness." JOY is an emotion that is very deep and truly so lasting. It is not only a felt emotion, but an expression which, when coupled with love, creates the closest feeling to perfection we can ever know.

JOY springs from within and is an internal experience, while happiness is something temporary. JOY is rooted from seeds that are planted in our life garden and that grow from memories and moments we have collected and placed into our invisible life backpacks. JOY brings calm to any storm and confidence to help us through and survive. JOY is a conscious commitment to be happy, no matter what we are going through, because JOY has a longer shelf life than mere happiness.

When I began my journey to wholeness in 2013, I could never have imagined that, not only would I survive my personal expedition, but when I was well, I would be tested again. I would have to live through a once-in-a-lifetime pandemic and witness a division among people that has not been seen in our country in generations. I could never have imagined that I would finally find my voice and begin to plant seeds to work on my true calling and purpose of becoming a teacher. (I will graduate at 54 years young). But nothing in the world can take away my JOY. I am constantly collecting anything I can, in any way I can, and at every moment in time.

There is a SONshine baby coming to my family. I am going to be a grandmother and there is no greater gift. He is the most perfect human being and we have not yet been formally introduced. We have met at several sonograms (mini-Zoom meetings, but these don't really count.) I will be present on his opening night and for this I can barely contain my JOY! As you can imagine, I have already stimulated the economy by decorating a nursery at our home for anytime he stops by. (Darryl is thrilled…Not!)

I AM OPEN. JOY teaches us to just open ourselves, to see farther than our eyes can look! I am Warrior Strong because of my journeys. I can travel with my warrior suit anywhere, through every situation, and know I can and will withstand whatever life may throw at me. Because now I use my Pantone decorated force field.

Now, after surviving this latest storm wearing my shiny warrior suit, what is my advice to people on their own roller coaster?

- *Smile twice as much as you frown. We have learned to smile with our eyes, as we wear masks. Do that.*

- *Always eat the dessert…even if it's gluten-free…eat the damn dessert! Drink the drinks. Just LIVE!*

- *People come into our lives for a reason, a season or a lifetime. Balance this with perspective, coupled with JOY for the time shared.*

- *Know your tribe, understand their value and appreciate the power of the net they hold you up in.*

- *Collect moments and memories as much as possible. You never know when you will need to pull them out to sustain you.*

- *We all start our lives with a five-burner stove, so respect everyone's kitchen and understand the rules of the refrigerator.*

- *The holy trinity has many meanings to many people. Define yours. Make this your mantra.*

- *Host as many dinner parties and house parties as you can. Go to live concerts, even if it's too loud. Watch big, huge sporting events, even if you're not a fan. Travel as much as you can, whenever you can, because one day it could all shut down.*

- *Do not waste time! Next to your health, it is the most precious gift you are given.*

- *Always look for the helpers…the energy givers.*

- *Warrior suits are waterproof and used for good. The energy givers will open and close your force field for calm and keep the crazy out. Decide what you give your energy to.*

- *JOY is waiting for you– beautiful pieces to be collected wherever you are–and living in the memories and moments.*

warrior strong

On May 21, 2021 we hosted our first dinner party in our home in 14 months. Everyone was vaccinated. We ate and drank and shared stories. We laughed for hours and shared a few tears. It was everything it was supposed to be at that exact moment in time. It felt right to share space once again with people who were part of my tribe—warriors, each one of them. It was JOY living out loud. I took a moment and photographed the memory and put it in my tiny backpack, took a deep exhale and shared a toast:

"Because of all of you, I laugh a little harder and cry a little less and smile a whole lot more. It's been at least 14 months since people gathered around our beautiful table and this moment is everything! So, please raise your glasses...here's to those who have seen us at our best and seen us at our worst and cannot tell the difference!"

"What is remembered, lives."

Nomadland, 2020

WHAT MAKES YOU WARRIOR STRONG?

_____

_____

_____

_____

_____

_____

_____

_____

warrior strong

www.ingramcontent.com/pod-product-compliance
Lightning Source LLC
Chambersburg PA
CBHW061513040426
42450CB00008B/1603